I. DIRECTOR'S PICKS

Cohen, Stephen F. *Soviet Fates and Lost Alternatives: From Stalinism to the New Cold War*. New York: Columbia UP, 2009.
(DK 266 .C587 2009)

Gvosdev, Nikolas K. and Christopher Marsh. *Russian Foreign Policy: Interests, Vectors, and Sectors*. Los Angeles: Sage, 2014.
(JZ 1616 .G86 2014)

Hill, Fiona and Clifford G. Gaddy. *Mr. Putin: Operative in the Kremlin*. Brookings Focus Books. Washington: Brookings, 2013.
(DK 510.766 .P87 H55 2013)

McFaul, Michael. "Moscow's Choice. "*Foreign Affairs* 93, no. 6(November 2014-December 2014): 167-71.

Mearsheimer, John J. "Mearsheimer Replies." *Foreign Affairs* 93, no. 6(November 2014-December 2014): 175-78.

_____. "Why the Ukraine Crisis Is the West's Fault." *Foreign Affairs* 93, no. 5(September 2014-October 2014): 77-89.

Sestanovich, Stephen. "How the West Has Won." *Foreign Affairs* 93, no. 6(November 2014-December 2014): 171-75.

Shevt?sova, Lilii a Fedorovna. *Putin's Russia*. Washington: Carnegie Endowment for International Peace, 2003.
(DK 510.763 .S492 2003)

Stent, Angela. *Limits of Partnership: U.S.-Russian Relations in the Twenty-First Century*. Princeton: Princeton UP, 2014.
(E 183.8 .R9 S836 2014)

Trenin, Dmitri. *The Ukraine Crisis and the Resumption of Great-Power Rivalry*. 2014.
(http://carnegie.ru/2014/07/09/ukraine-crisis-and-resumption-of-great-power-rivalry/hfgs)

Tsygankov, Andrei P. *Russia's Foreign Policy: Change and Continuity in National Identity*. 3rd ed. Lanham: Rowman, 2013.
(DK 510.764 .T785 2013)

II. GLOBAL FOREIGN POLICY WITH DIPLOMACY
Books, Government Documents, and Report Literature

Ahrari, Mohammed E. *The Great Powers Versus the Hegemon*. Basingstoke, Hampshire: Palgrave Macmillan, 2011.
(JZ 1312 .A3 2011)

Aktürk, Sener. *Regimes of Ethnicity and Nationhood in Germany, Russia, and Turkey*. Problems of International Politics. New York: Cambridge UP, 2012.
(JN 34.7 .A57 2012)

Bedeski, Robert, and Niklas Swanstrom, eds. *Eurasia's Ascent in Energy and Geopolitics: Rivalry or Partnership for China, Russia and Central Asia?* Routledge Contemporary Asia Series; 38. New York: Routledge, 2012.
(HF 3630.2 .Z7 C628 2012)

Blank, Stephen, ed. *Central Asia after 2014*. Carlisle: U.S. Army War College, Strategic Studies Institute, 2013.
(REPORT LITERATURE   AD-A588 031)
(http://www.strategicstudiesinstitute.army.mil/pubs/download.cfm?q=1175)

Blank, Stephen J., ed. *Perspectives on Russian Foreign Policy*. Strategic Studies Institute monograph. Carlisle: U.S. Army War College, Strategic Studies Institute, 2012.
(REPORT LITERATURE   AD-A565 485)
(<http://www.strategicstudiesinstitute.army.mil/pubs/display.cfm?pubID=1115>)

_____. *Russia in the Arctic*. SSI Monograph. Carlisle, PA: U.S. Army War College, Strategic Studies Institute, 2011.
(REPORT LITERATURE AD-A547 491)
(http://www.strategicstudiesinstitute.army.mil/pdffiles/PUB1073.pdf)

Chun, Kwang Ho. *The BRICs Superpower Challenge: Foreign and Security Policy Analysis*. Burlington: Ashgate, 2013.
(JZ 1310 .C495 2013)

Delcour, Laure. *Shaping the Post-Soviet Space? EU Policies and Approaches to Region-Building*. Farnham, Surrey; Burlington: Ashgate, 2011.
(JZ 1570 .A57 D45 2011)

Donaldson, Robert H. and Joseph L. Nogee. *The Foreign Policy of Russia: Changing Systems, Enduring Interests*. 4th ed. Armonk: M.E. Sharpe, 2009.
(DK 266.45 .D66 2009)

Giles, Keir. *Russian Interests in Sub-Saharan Africa.* Letort Papers. Carlisle: U.S. Army War College, Strategic Studies Institute, 2013.
(REPORT LITERATURE   AD-A583 576)
(http://www.strategicstudiesinstitute.army.mil/pubs/download.cfm?q=1169)

Gvosdev, Nikolas K. and Christopher Marsh. *Russian Foreign Policy: Interests, Vectors, and Sectors.* Los Angeles: Sage, 2014.
(JZ 1616 .G86 2014)

Hachigian, Nina and Mona Sutphen. *The Next American Century: How the U.S. Can Thrive As Other Powers Rise.* New York: Simon & Schuster, 2010.
(E 895 .H33 2010)

Jersild, Austin. *The Sino-Soviet Alliance: An International History.* New Cold War history. Chapel Hill: U of North Carolina P, 2014.
(DS 740.5 .S65 J47 2014)

Jervis, Robert. *Perception and Misperception in International Politics.* Princeton: Princeton UP, 1976.
(JX 1291 .J47)

Kanet, Roger E. *Russian Foreign Policy in the 21st Century.* Houndmills, Basingstoke, Hampshire; New York: Palgrave Macmillan, 2011.
(DK 510.764 .R865 2011)

Kanet, Roger E., and Remi Piet, eds. *Shifting Priorities in Russia's Foreign and Security Policy.* Global Interdisciplinary Studies. Burlington: Ashgate, 2014.
(JZ 1616 .S55 2014)

Kundu, Nivedita Das, ed. *Russia-India-China: Evolution of Geo-Political Strategic Trends.* New Delhi: Academic Foundation in association with Indian Council of World Affairs, 2010.
(DK 510.764 .R8524 2010)

Lai, David. *Asia-Pacific: A Strategic Assessment.* Carlisle: U. S. Army War College, Strategic Studies Institute, 2013.
(REPORT LITERATURE   ADA 579509)
(<http://www.strategicstudiesinstitute.army.mil/pubs/display.cfm?pubID=1155>)

Lennon, Alexander T. J., and Amanda Kozlowski, eds. *Global Powers in the 21st Century: Strategies and Relations.* Washington Quarterly Reader. Cambridge: MIT P, 2008.
(JZ 1313 .G56 2008)

Lo, Bobo. *Russia and the New World Disorder.* Washington; London: Brookings Institution; Chatham House, 2014.
(On order)

Malashenko, Alexey. *The Fight for Influence: Russia in Central Asia.* Washington:
    Carnegie Endowment for International Peace, 2014.
    (DK 857.75 .R8 M3613 2013)

Mangala, Jack, ed. *Africa and the New World Era: From Humanitarianism to a Strategic
    View.* New York: Palgrave Macmillan, 2010.
    (DT 31 .A435 2010)

Mankoff, Jeffrey. *Russian Foreign Policy: The Return of Great Power Politics.* 2nd ed.
    Council on Foreign Relations. Lanham: Rowman, 2012.
    (JZ 1616 .M36 2012)

Nau, Henry R., and Deepa Mary Ollapally, eds. *Worldviews of Aspiring Powers:
    Domestic Foreign Policy Debates in China, India, Iran, Japan, and Russia.* New
    York: Oxford UP, 2012.
    (JZ 1310 .W68 2012)

Parker, John W. *Russia's Revival: Ambitions, Limitations, and Opportunities for the
    United States.* Institute for National Strategic Studies Strategic Perspectives ; 3.
    Washington: National Defense U, 2011.
    (REPORT LITERATURE   AD-A546 683)
    (http://ndupress.ndu.edu/Portals/68/Documents/stratperspective/inss/Strategic-
    Perspectives-3.pdf)

Pursiainen, Christer, ed. *At the Crossroads of Post-Communist Modernisation: Russia
    and China in Comparative Perspective.* New York: Palgrave Macmillan, 2012.

Radchenko, Sergey. *Unwanted Visionaries: The Soviet Failure in Asia at the End of the
    Cold War.* Oxford Studies in International History. New York: Oxford UP, 2014.
    (DK 68 .R28 2014)

Rozman, Gilbert. *Sino-Russian Challenge to the World Order: National Identities,
    Bilateral Relations, and East Versus West in the 2010s.* Stanford: Stanford UP,
    2014.
    (DK 68.7 .C5 R69 2014)

Rumer, Eugene B. *Russian Foreign Policy Beyond Putin.* Adelphi Papers; no. 390.
    Abingdon; New York: Routledge for IISS, 2007.
    (U 162 .A23 no.390)

Sarotte, M. E. *1989: The Struggle to Create Post-Cold War Europe.* Princeton Studies
    in International History and Politics. Princeton: Princeton UP, 2009.
    (D 860 .S2694 2009)

Sherr, James. *Hard Diplomacy and Soft Coercion: Russia's Influence Abroad.* London:
    Chatham House, Royal Institute of International Affairs, 2013.
    (DK 66 .S517 2013)

Smith, Martin A. *Power in the Changing Global Order: The US, Russia and China*.
Cambridge; Malden: Polity, 2012.
(JZ 1310 .S64 2012)

Smith, S. A. (Stephen Anthony), Amelia Hadfield, and Timothy Dunne, eds. *Foreign Policy: Theories, Actors, Cases*. 2nd ed. Oxford: Oxford UP, 2012.
(JZ 1305 .F67 2012)

Thornton, William H. *Toward a Geopolitics of Hope*. Thousand Oaks: Sage, 2012.
(JC 319 .T525 2012)

Trenin, Dmitrii. *Post-Imperium: A Eurasian Story*. Washington: Carnegie Endowment for International Peace, 2011.
(DK 510.76 .T73 2011)

Tsygankov, Andrei P. *Russia and the West from Alexander to Putin: Honor in International Relations*. Cambridge: Cambridge UP, 2014.
(JZ 1615 .T77 2014)

_____. *Russia's Foreign Policy: Change and Continuity in National Identity*. 2nd ed. Lanham: Rowman, 2010.
(DK 510.764 .T785 2010)

_____. *Russia's Foreign Policy: Change and Continuity in National Identity*. 3rd ed. Lanham: Rowman, 2013.
(DK 510.764 .T785 2013)

JOURNALS

Allison, Roy. "Russia and Syria: Explaining Alignment with a Regime in Crisis." *International Affairs* 89, no. 4(July 2013): 795-823.

Berryman, John. "Geopolitics and Russian Foreign Policy." *International Politics* 49, no. 4(July 2012): 530-44.

Chang, Gordon G. "China and Russia." *World Affairs* 176, no. 6(March 2014-April 2014): 17-30.

Demidov, Andrey V. "Russia's Foreign Policy in the Emerging Global Order." *Journal of European Studies* 28, no. 2(December 2012): n/a.

Deyermond, Ruth. "The Republican Challenge to Obama's Russia Policy." *Survival* 54, no. 5(October 2012-November 2012): 67-92.

Dodds, Klaus. "The Ilulissat Declaration (2008): The Arctic States, "Law of the Sea," and Arctic Ocean." *SAIS Review of International Affairs* 33, no. 2(Summer 2013-Fall 2013): 45-55.

Glasser, Susan B. "Minister No." *Foreign Policy* 200(May 2013-June 2013): 52-62.

Kaczmarski, Marcin. "Domestic Sources of Russia's China Policy." *Problems of Post-Communism* 59, no. 2(March 2012-April 2012): 3-17.

Kant, Roger E. "Russia in the New International Order: Theories, Arguments and Debates Introduction." *International Politics* 49, no. 4(July 2012): 393-99.

Katz, Mark N. "Russia and the Conflict in Syria: Four Myths." *Middle East Policy* 20, no. 2(Summer 2013): 38-46.

Kireeva, Anna. "Russia's East Asia Policy: New Opportunities and Challenges." *Perceptions* 17, no. 4(Winter 2012): 49-78.

Kubyshkin, Aleksandr and Aleksandr Sergunin. "The Problem of the "Special Path" in Russian Foreign Policy (From the 1990s to the Early Twenty-First Century)." *Russian Politics and Law* 50, no. 6(November 2012-December 2012): 7-18.

Kuchins, Andrew C. and Igor A. Zevelev. "Russian Foreign Policy: Continuity in Change." *Washington Quarterly* 35, no. 1(February 2012): 147-61.

Lannon, Gregory P. "Russia's New Look Army Reforms and Russian Foreign Policy." *Journal of Slavic Military Studies* 24, no. 1(January 2011-March 2011): 26-54.

Lukin, Alexander. "Eurasian Integration and the Clash of Values." *Survival* 56, no. 3(June 2014-July 2014): 43-60.

_____. "What the Kremlin Is Thinking: Putin's Vision for Eurasia." *Foreign Affairs* 93, no. 4(July 2014-August 2014): 85-93.

Mearsheimer, John J. "Why the Ukraine Crisis Is the West's Fault." *Foreign Affairs* 93, no. 5(September 2014-October 2014): 77-89.

Moshes, Arkady. "Russia's European Policy Under Medvedev: How Sustainable Is a New Compromise?" *International Affairs* 88, no. 1(January 2012): 17-30.

Ostrow, Rachel. "Pax Russica: Russia's Role in the Race for the Arctic." *SAIS Review of International Affairs* 33, no. 2(Summer 2013-Fall 2013): 57-9.

Ratti, Luca. "'Resetting' NATO–Russia Relations: A Realist Appraisal Two Decades after the USSR." *Journal of Slavic Military Studies* 26, no. 2(April 2013-June 2013): 141-61.

Rutland, Peter. "Still Out in the Cold? Russia's Place in a Globalizing World." *Communist and Post-Communist Studies* 45, no. 3-4(Sep-Dec2012): 343-54.

Sarotte, Mary Elise. "A Broken Promise?" *Foreign Affairs* 93, no. 5(September 2014-October 2014): 90-7.

Surovell, Jeffrey. "Deception and Farce in Post-Soviet Russian Policy Vis-ą-Vis NATO's Expansion." *Journal of Slavic Military Studies* 25, no. 2(2012): 162-82.

Sussex, Matthew. "Twenty Years after the Fall: Continuity and Change in Russian Foreign and Security Policy." *Global Change, Peace & Security* 24, no. 2(June 2012): 203-17.

Yu, Bin. "China-Russia Relations: Summer Heat and Sino-Russian Strategizing." *Comparative Connections (E-Journal)* 15, no. 2(October 2013): 1-12.

Ziegler, Charles E. "Conceptualizing Sovereignty in Russian Foreign Policy: Realist and Constructivist Perspectives." *International Politics* 49, no. 4(July 2012): 400-17.

III. FOREIGN POLICY DOMESTIC INFLUENCES INCLUDING POLITICS
Books, Government Documents, and Report Literature

Arutunyas, Anna. *The Putin Mystique: Inside Russia's Power Cult*. North Hampton: Olive Branch, 2014.
(DK 510.766 .P87 A78 2014b)

Bennetts, Marc. *Kicking the Kremlin: Russia's New Dissidents and the Battle to Topple Putin*. London: Oneworld, 2014.
(JN 6581 .B46 2014)

Blank, Stephen, ed. *Can Russia Reform? Economic, Political, and Military Perspectives*. Strategic Studies Institute Monograph. Carlisle: U.S. Army War College; Strategic Studies Institute, 2012.
(REPORT LITERATURE   AD-A561 500)
(http://www.strategicstudiesinstitute.army.mil/pubs/display.cfm?pubID=1111)

_____. *Politics and Economics in Putin's Russia*. Carlisle: U.S. Army War College, Strategic Studies Institute, 2013.
(REPORT LITERATURE AD-A590 426)
(http://permanent.access.gpo.gov/gpo45165/pub1180%5b1%5d.pdf)

Boterbloem, Kees. *A History of Russia and Its Empire: From Mikhail Romanov to Vladimir Putin*. Lanham: Rowman, 2014.
(DK 40 .B596 2014)

Cohen, Stephen F. *Soviet Fates and Lost Alternatives: From Stalinism to the New Cold War*. New York: Columbia UP, 2009.
(DK 266 .C587 2009)

English, Robert D. *Russia and the Idea of the West: Gorbachev, Intellectuals, and the End of the Cold War*. New York: Columbia UP, 2000.
(DK 274 .E54 2000)

Feifer, Gregory. *Russians: The People behind the Power*. New York; Boston: Twelve, 2014.
(DK 510.762 .F45 2014)

Gessen, Masha. *The Man without a Face: The Unlikely Rise of Vladimir Putin*. New York: Riverhead, 2012.
(DK 510.766 .P87 G47 2012)

Hill, Fiona and Clifford G. Gaddy. *Mr. Putin: Operative in the Kremlin*. Brookings Focus Books. Washington: Brookings, 2013.
(DK 510.766 .P87 H55 2013)

Krickus, Richard J. *Russia after Putin*. Carlisle: U.S. Army War College, Strategic
   Studies Institute, 2014.
   (REPORT LITERATURE AD –A601 840)
   (<http://www.strategicstudiesinstitute.army.mil/pubs/display.cfm?pubID=1200>)

Lucas, Edward. *The New Cold War: Putin's Russia and the Threat to the West*. New
   York: Palgrave Macmillan, 2008.
   (JZ 1616 .L83 2008)

Medvedev, Sergei. *Rethinking the National Interest: Putin's Turn in Russian Foreign
   Policy*. Marshall Center papers ; no. 6. Garmisch-Partenkirchen: George C.
   Marshall European Center for Security Studies, 2004.
   (Gov Doc D 1.111/2:6)(DK 510.764 .M22 2004)
   (http://permanent.access.gpo.gov/lps61241/mc-paper_6-en.pdf)

Mickiewicz, Ellen. *No Illusions: The Voices of Russia's Future Leaders*. Oxford, New
   York: Oxford UP, 2014.
   (JN 6695 .M528 2014)

Plokhy, Serhil. *The Last Empire: The Final Days of the Soviet Union*. New York: Basic
   Books, 2014.
   (DK 286 .P57 2014)

Roberts, Sean P. *Putin's United Russia Party*. London; New York: Routledge, 2012.
   (JN 6699 .A8 P6545 2012)

Schrad, Mark Lawrence. *Vodka Politics: Alcohol, Autocracy, and the Secret History of
   the Russian State*. Oxford; New York: Oxford UP, 2014.
   (HV 5513 .S37 2014)

Sherr, James. *Hard Diplomacy and Soft Coercion: Russia's Influence Abroad*. London:
   Chatham House, Royal Institute of International Affairs, 2013.
   (DK 66 .S517 2013)

Shevt?sova, Lilii a Fedorovna. *Putin's Russia*. Washington: Carnegie Endowment for
   International Peace, 2003.
   (DK 510.763 .S492 2003)

Smith, Jeremy. *Red Nations: The Nationalities Experience in and after the USSR*.
   Cambridge; New York: Cambridge UP, 2013.
   (JN 6520 .S8 S59 2013)

Stuermer, Michael. *Putin and the Rise of Russia*. New York: Pegasus, 2009.
   (DK 510.763 .S78 2009)

Thompson, John M. *Russia and the Soviet Union: A Historical Introduction from the
   Kievan State to the Present*. 7th ed. Boulder: Westview, 2013.
   (DK 40 .T48 2013)

Treisman, Daniel. *The Return: Russia's Journey from Gorbachev to Medvedev*. New York: Free, 2011.
(JN 6695 .T74 2011)

United States. Congress. House. Committee on Foreign Affairs. *Russia 2012: Increased Repression, Rampant Corruption, Assisting Rogue Regimes*. Hearing. 112th Cong., 2d sess. Washington: GPO, 2012.
(Gov Doc Y 4.F 76/1:112-141)

Van Herpen, Marcel H. *Putin's Wars: The Rise of Russia's New Imperialism*. Lanham: Rowman & Littlefield, 2014.
(DK 510.764 .H47 2014)

Zimmerman, William. *Ruling Russia: Authoritarianism From the Revolution to Putin*. Princeton: Princeton UP, 2014.
(JN 6531 .Z56 2014)

JOURNALS

Biberman, Yelen. "The Politics of Diplomatic Service Reform in Post-Soviet Russia." *Political Science Quarterly* 126, no. 4(2012): 669-80.

Burke-White, William W. "Crimea and the International Legal Order." *Survival* 56, no. 4(August 2014-September 2014): 65-80.

Freire, Maria Raquel. "Russian Foreign Policy in the Making: The Linkage between Internal Dynamics and the External Context." *International Politics* 49, no. 4(July 2012): 466-81.

Galeotti, Mark and Andrew S. Bowen. "Putin's Empire of the Mind." *Foreign Policy* 206(May 2014-June 2014): 16-9.

Hahn, Gordon M. "Russia in 2012: From "Thaw" and "Reset" to "Freeze"." *Asian Survey* 53, no. 1(January 2013-February 2013): 214-23.

Kara-Murza, Vladimir V. "Kremlin Crooks." *World Affairs* 176, no. 2(July 2013-August 2013): 56-63.

_____. "Politics in Russia." *World Affairs* 176, no. 5(January 2014-February 2014): 47-54.

_____. "Russia's Local Elections." *World Affairs* 175, no. 3(September 2012-October 2012): 53-60.

Katz, Mark. "What Would a Democratic Russian Foreign Policy Look Like?" *New Zealand International Review* 37, no. 2(March 2012-April 2012): 2-6.

Kaylan, Melik. "Kremlin Values." *World Affairs* 177, no. 1(May 2014-June 2014): 9-17.

Khrushcheva, Nina L. "Inside Vladimir Putin's Mind." *World Affairs* 177, no. 2(July 2014-August 2014): 17-24.

Kipp, Jacob W. "'Smart' Defense from New Threats: Future War from a Russian Perspective: Back to the Future after the War on Terror." *Journal of Slavic Military Studies* 27, no. 1(January 2014-March 2014): 36-62.

Kuchins, Andrew C. and Igor A. Zevelev. "Russian Foreign Policy: Continuity in Change." *Washington Quarterly* 35, no. 1(February 2012): 147-61.

Laqueur, Walter. "After the Fall: Russia in Search of a New Ideology." *World Affairs* 176, no. 6(March 2014-April 2014): 71-7.

McLure, Jason. "Russia in Turmoil." *CQ Researcher* 6, no. 4(February 2012): 81-104. (CQ Researcher Online)

Monaghan, Andrew. "Putin's Russia: Shaping a 'Grand Strategy'?" *International Affairs* 89, no. 5(September 2013): 1221-236.

_____. "The Vertikal: Power and Authority in Russia." *International Affairs* 88, no. 1(January 2012): 1-16.

Morozov, Viatcheslav. "Subaltern Empire? Toward a Postcolonial Approach to Russian Foreign Policy." *Problems of Post-Communism* 60, no. 6(November 2013-December 2013): 16-28.

Petersson, Bo. "The Eternal Great Power Meets the Recurring Times of Troubles: Twin Political Myths in Contemporary Russian Politics." *European Studies* 30(2013): 301-26, 9.

Rubin, Michael. "Why 'Reset' Failed." *World Affairs* 177, no. 2(July 2014-August 2014): 74-81.

Saari, Sinikukka. "Russia's Post-Orange Revolution Strategies to Increase Its Influence in Former Soviet Republics: Public Diplomacy Po Russkii." *Europe-Asia Studies* 66, no. 1(January 2014): 50-66.

Sakwa, Richard. "The Problem of 'the International' in Russian Identity Formation." *International Politics* 49, no. 4(July 2012): 449-65.

_____. "Russia: From Stalemate to Crisis?" *Brown Journal of World Affairs* 19, no. 1(Fall 2012-Winter 2012): 231-46.

Shevtsova, Lilia. "The Russia Factor." *Journal of Democracy* 25, no. 3(July 2014).

Simao, Licinia. "Do Leaders Still Decide? The Role of Leadership in Russian Foreign Policymaking." *International Politics* 49, no. 4(July 2012): 482-97.

Sorokin, Vladimir. "Let the Past Collapse on Time." *New York Review of Books* 61, no. 8(May 2014): 4-6 .

Weiss, Michael. "Rights in Russia." *World Affairs* 176, no. 4(November 2013-December 2013): 72-80.

Wieclawski, Jacek. "Contemporary Realism and the Foreign Policy of the Russian Federation." *International Journal of Business and Social Science* 2, no. 1(January 2011): 170-179.

IV. RUSSIA'S RELATIONS WITH USA
Books, Government Documents, and Report Literature

Arutunyas, Anna. *The Putin Mystique: Inside Russia's Power Cult*. North Hampton: Olive Branch, 2014.
(DK 510.766 .P87 A78 2014b)

Bennetts, Marc. *Kicking the Kremlin: Russia's New Dissidents and the Battle to Topple Putin*. London: Oneworld, 2014.
(JN 6581 .B46 2014)

Blank, Stephen, ed. *Can Russia Reform? Economic, Political, and Military Perspectives*. Strategic Studies Institute Monograph. Carlisle: U.S. Army War College; Strategic Studies Institute, 2012.
(REPORT LITERATURE AD-A561 500)
(http://www.strategicstudiesinstitute.army.mil/pubs/display.cfm?pubID=1111)

_____. *Politics and Economics in Putin's Russia*. Carlisle: U.S. Army War College, Strategic Studies Institute, 2013.
(REPORT LITERATURE AD-A590 426)
(http://permanent.access.gpo.gov/gpo45165/pub1180%5b1%5d.pdf)

Boterbloem, Kees. *A History of Russia and Its Empire: From Mikhail Romanov to Vladimir Putin*. Lanham: Rowman & Littlefield, 2014.
(DK 40 .B596 2014)

Cohen, Stephen F. *Soviet Fates and Lost Alternatives: From Stalinism to the New Cold War*. New York: Columbia UP, 2009.
(DK 266 .C587 2009)

English, Robert D. *Russia and the Idea of the West: Gorbachev, Intellectuals, and the End of the Cold War*. New York: Columbia UP, 2000.
(DK 274 .E54 2000)

Feifer, Gregory. *Russians: The People behind the Power*. New York; Boston: Twelve, 2014.
(DK 510.762 .F45 2014)

Gessen, Masha. *The Man without a Face: The Unlikely Rise of Vladimir Putin*. New York: Riverhead, 2012.
(DK 510.766 .P87 G47 2012)

Hill, Fiona and Clifford G. Gaddy. *Mr. Putin: Operative in the Kremlin*. Brookings Focus Books. Washington: Brookings, 2013.
(DK 510.766 .P87 H55 2013)

Kopstein, Jeffrey, and Mark Irving Lichbach, eds. *Comparative Politics: Interests, Identities, and Institutions in a Changing Global Order*. 3rd ed. New York: Cambridge UP, 2009.
(JF 51 .C6235 2009)

Krickus, Richard J. *Russia after Putin*. Carlisle: U.S. Army War College, Strategic Studies Institute, 2014.
(REPORT LITERATURE AD-A601 840)
(<http://www.strategicstudiesinstitute.army.mil/pubs/display.cfm?pubID=1200>)

Lucas, Edward. *The New Cold War: Putin's Russia and the Threat to the West*. New York: Palgrave Macmillan, 2008.
(JZ 1616 .L83 2008)

Medvedev, Sergei. *Rethinking the National Interest: Putin's Turn in Russian Foreign Policy*. Marshall Center papers; no. 6. Garmisch-Partenkirchen: George C. Marshall European Center for Security Studies, 2004.
(Gov Doc D 1.111/2:6) (DK 510.764 .M22 2004)
(http://permanent.access.gpo.gov/lps61241/mc-paper_6-en.pdf)

Mickiewicz, Ellen. *No Illusions: The Voices of Russia's Future Leaders*. Oxford, New York: Oxford UP, 2014.
(JN 6695 .M528 2014)

Plokhy, Serhil. *The Last Empire: The Final Days of the Soviet Union*. New York: Basic Books, 2014.
(DK 286 .P57 2014)

Roberts, Sean P. *Putin's United Russia Party*. London; New York: Routledge, 2012.
(JN 6699 .A8 P6545 2012)

Schrad, Mark Lawrence. *Vodka Politics: Alcohol, Autocracy, and the Secret History of the Russian State*. Oxford; New York: Oxford UP, 2014.
(HV 5513 .S37 2014)

Sherr, James. *Hard Diplomacy and Soft Coercion: Russia's Influence Abroad*. London: Chatham House, Royal Institute of International Affairs, 2013.
(DK 66 .S517 2013)

Shevt?sova, Lilii a Fedorovna. *Putin's Russia*. Washington: Carnegie Endowment for International Peace, 2003.
(DK 510.763 .S492 2003)

Smith, Jeremy. *Red Nations: The Nationalities Experience in and after the USSR*. Cambridge; New York: Cambridge UP, 2013.
(JN 6520 .S8 S59 2013)

Stuermer, Michael. *Putin and the Rise of Russia*. New York: Pegasus, 2009.
(DK 510.763 .S78 2009)

Thompson, John M. *Russia and the Soviet Union: A Historical Introduction from the Kievan State to the Present*. 7th ed. Boulder: Westview, 2013.
(DK 40 .T48 2013)

Treisman, Daniel. *The Return: Russia's Journey from Gorbachev to Medvedev*. New York: Free, 2011.
(JN 6695 .T74 2011)

United States. Congress. House. Committee on Foreign Affairs. *Russia 2012: Increased Repression, Rampant Corruption, Assisting Rogue Regimes*. Hearing. 112th Cong., 2d sess. Washington: GPO, 2012.
(Gov Doc Y 4.F 76/1:112-141)

Van Herpen, Marcel H. *Putin's Wars: The Rise of Russia's New Imperialism*. Lanham: Rowman, 2014.
(DK 510.764 .H47 2014)

Zimmerman, William. *Ruling Russia: Authoritarianism from the Revolution to Putin*. Princeton: Princeton UP, 2014.
(JN 6531 .Z56 2014)

JOURNALS

"A Summary of Activities of the US/Soviet-Russian Joint Working Group on Space Biology and Medicine." *Acta Astronautica* 67, no. 7-8(October 2010-November 2010): 649-58.

Blank, Stephen. "Resets, Russia, and Iranian Proliferation." *Mediterranean Quarterly* 23, no. 1(Winter 2012): 14-38.

Chadova-Devlen, Elena. "Whose Interests? US-Russian Foreign Policy Controversies in Russian American Ethnic Press." *International Studies Perspectives* 15, no. 1(February 2014): 36-53.

Cimbala, Stephen J. "Missile Defense Malpractice: U.S.-Russian Relations and Nuclear Fallacy." *Journal of Slavic Military Studies* 25, no. 3(July 2012-September 2012): 269-83.

Dorofeev, Sergei. "Russian and U.S. Interests in Central Asia." *Russian Politics and Law* 51, no. 1(January 2013-February 2013): 7-24.

Gustafson, K. C. "Echo of Empires: Russia's Inheritance of Byzantine Security Culture." *Journal of Slavic Military Studies* 23, no. 4(Oct-Dec2010): 574-96.

Herspring, Dale R. "Creating Shared Responsibility through Respect for Military Culture: The Russian and American Cases." *Public Administration Review* 71, no. 4(July 2011-August 2011): 519-29.

Katel, Peter. "U.S. Global Engagement." *CQ Researcher* 24, no. 19(May 2014): 433-55.

Kuchins, Andrew C. and Igor A. Zevelev. "Russian Foreign Policy: Continuity in Change." *Washington Quarterly* 35, no. 1(February 2012): 147-61.

Legvold, Robert. "Managing the New Cold War." *Foreign Affairs* 93, no. 4(July 2014-August 2014): 74-84.

Logsdon, John M. and James R. Millar. "US-Russian Cooperation in Human Spaceflight: Assessing the Impacts." *Space Policy* 17, no. 3(August 2001): 171-78.

Roberts, Kari. "Detente 2.0? The Meaning of Russia's "Reset" with the United States." *International Studies Perspectives* 15, no. 1(February 2014): 1-18.

V. RUSSIA SPACE HISTORY
Books, Governmant Documents, and Report Literature

Andrews, James T. *Red Cosmos: K.E. Tsiolkovskii, Grandfather of Soviet Rocketry*. Centennial of Flight Series, no.18. College Station: Texas A&M UP, 2009. (TL 789.85 .T8 A53 2009)

Andrews, James T., and Asif A. Siddiqu, eds. *Into the Cosmos: Space Exploration and Soviet Culture*. Series in Russian and East European Studies. Pittsburgh: U of Pittsburgh P, 2011. (TLE 1031.5 .I61 2011)

Harvey, Brian. *The Rebirth of the Russian Space Program: 50 Years after Sputnik, New Frontiers*. Springer-Praxis Books in Space Exploration. New York: Springer, 2007. (TLE 1031.5 .H3413 2007)

_____. *Russian Planetary Exploration: History, Development, Legacy, Prospects*. Springer-Praxis Books in Space Exploration. Berlin; New York: Springer, 2007. (TLE 1031.5 .H3411 2007)

Harvey, Brian and Olga Zakutnyaya. *Russian Space Probes: Scientific Discoveries and Future Missions*. Springer-Praxis Books in Space Exploration. New York: Springer, 2011. (TLE 1031.5 .H3414 2011)

Hendrickx, Bart and Bert Vis. *Energiya-Buran: The Soviet Space Shuttle*. Springer-Praxis Books in Space Exploration. Berlin; New York: Springer, 2007. (TLE 1123.5 .H498 2007)

Maurer, Eva. *Soviet Space Culture: Cosmic Enthusiasm in Socialist Societies*. Houndmills, Basingstoke, Hampshire; New York: Palgrave Macmillan, 2011. (TLE 1031.5 .S729 2011)

Moltz, James Clay. *The Politics of Space Security: Strategic Restraint and the Pursuit of National Interests*. 2nd ed. Stanford: Stanford UP, 2011. (TLE 1037 .M729 2011)

Phelan, Dominic, ed. *Cold War Space Sleuths: The Untold Secrets of the Soviet Space Program*. New York: Springer, 2013. (TLE 1031.5 .C688 2013)

Robertson, Ann E. *Militarization of Space*. Global Issues. New York: Facts on File, 2011. (UGK 1012 .N158 2011)

Smith, Michael G. *Rockets and Revolution: A Cultural History of Early Spaceflight*. Lincoln: U of Nebraska P, 2014.
(TL 788.5 .S5835 2014)

JOURNALS

"A Summary of Activities of the US/Soviet-Russian Joint Working Group on Space Biology and Medicine." *Acta Astronautica* 67, no. 7-8(October 2010-November 2010): 649-58.

Baird, Mark A. "Maintaining Space Situational Awareness and Taking It to the Next Level." *Air & Space Power Journal* 27, no. 5(September 2013-October 2013): 50-72.

Faith, G. Ryan. "Future of Space." *World Affairs* 175, no. 3(September 2012-October 2012): 82-7.

Gagnon, Bruce K. "U.S. Space Technology for Controlling China and Russia." *Peace Review* 22, no. 1(January 2010-March 2010): 17-24.

Gottemoeller, R. and BAS. "Rose Gottemoeller: Getting to Yes." *Bulletin of the Atomic Scientists* 67, no. 6(November 2011-December 2011): 1-8.

Graham Jr., Thomas. "The Essentiality of Effective Verification: From Sputnik to the Space Station." *Problems of Post-Communism* 53, no. 2(March 2006-April 2006): 17-29.

Hughes, James H. "Confusion over Space." *The Journal of Social, Political and Economic Studies* 36, no. 1(Spring 2011): 3-54.

Krasnov, Aleksei. "Risks in International Space Activities." *International Affairs: A Russian Journal of World Politics, Diplomacy & International Relations* 48, no. 4(2002): 68-75.

Logsdon, John M. and James R. Millar. "US-Russian Cooperation in Human Spaceflight: Assessing the Impacts." *Space Policy* 17, no. 3(August 2001): 171-78.

Manber, Jeffrey. "Russian--American Space Miscommunication: A Study in Missed Opportunities." *Space Policy* 16, no. 1(February 2000): 3-6.

Moltz, James Clay. "The Past, Present, and Future of Space Security." *Brown Journal of World Affairs* 14, no. 1(Fall 2007-Winter 2007): 187-95.

Pouzanov, S. "Russia-U.S. Space Partnership." *International Affairs: A Russian Journal of World Politics, Diplomacy & International Relations.* 57, no. 1(2011): 238-50.

Yakovenko, A. "The Intergovernmental Agreement on the International Space Station."
Space Policy 15, no. 2(May 1999): 79-86.

VI. MILITARY AND SECURITY RELATIONS
Books, Government Documents, and Report Literature

Arbatov, Aleksei Georgievich, Vladimir Dvorkin, and Vladimir Evseev. *Beyond Nuclear Deterrence: Transforming the U.S.-Russian Equation.* Washington: Carnegie Endowment for International Peace, 2006.
(JZ 5665 .A73 2006)

Baev, Pavel. *Russian Energy Policy and Military Power: Putin's Quest for Greatness.* Contemporary Security Studies. London; New York: Routledge, 2008.
(DK 510.763 .B344 2008)

Blank, Stephen, ed. *Can Russia Reform? Economic, Political, and Military Perspectives.* Strategic Studies Institute Monograph. Carlisle: U.S. Army War College; Strategic Studies Institute, 2012.
(REPORT LITERATURE   AD-A561 500)
(http://www.strategicstudiesinstitute.army.mil/pubs/display.cfm?pubID=1111)

_____. *Politics and Economics in Putin's Russia.* Carlisle: U.S. Army War College, Strategic Studies Institute, 2013.
(REPORT LITERATURE AD-A590 426)
(http://permanent.access.gpo.gov/gpo45165/pub1180%5b1%5d.pdf)

_____. *Russia and the Current State of Arms Control.* Carlisle: U.S. Army War College, Strategic Studies Institute, 2012.
(REPORT LITERATURE   AD-A565 482)
(http://www.strategicstudiesinstitute.army.mil/pubs/download.cfm?q=1119)

Blank, Stephen J., and Richard Weitz, eds. *The Russian Military Today and Tomorrow: Essays in Memory of Mary Fitzgerald.* Carlisle: U.S. Army War College, Strategic Studies Institute, 2010.
(REPORT LITERATURE AD-A525 166) (http://handle.dtic.mil/100.2/ADA525166)

Blank, Stephen J., ed. *Russian Military Politics and Russia's 2010 Defense Doctrine.* Carlisle: U.S. Army War College, Strategic Studies Institute, 2011.
(REPORT LITERATURE   AD-A539 964)
(http://www.strategicstudiesinstitute.army.mil/pdffiles/PUB1050.pdf)

Busch, Nathan E. and Daniel Joyner. *Combating Weapons of Mass Destruction: The Future of International Nonproliferation Policy.* Studies in Security and International Affairs. Athens: U of Georgia P, 2009.
(JZ 5675 .C65 2009)

Carr, Jeffrey and Lewis Shepherd. *Inside Cyber Warfare.* Sebastopol, CA: O'Reilly Media, 2009.
(U 163 .C37 2009)

Cimbala, Stephen J. and Peter Jacob Rainow. *Russia and Postmodern Deterrence: Military Power and Its Challenges for Security*. Issues in Twenty-First Century Warfare. Washington: Potomac, 2007.
(UA 770 .C5626 2007)

Cohen, Ariel. *Russia's Counterinsurgency in North Caucasus: Performance and Consequences; the Strategic Threat of Religious Extremism and Moscow's Response*. Carlisle: U.S. Army War College, Strategic Studies Institute, 2014.
(REPORT LITERATURE AD-A597 804)
(<http://www.strategicstudiesinstitute.army.mil/pubs/display.cfm?pubID=1189>)

Cuccia, Phillip R. *Implications of a Changing NATO*. Carlisle: U.S. Army War College, Strategic Studies institute, 2010.
(REPORT LITERATURE   AD-A520 868)
(http://www.strategicstudiesinstitute.army.mil/pdffiles/PUB990.pdf)

Davies, Philip H. J., and Kristian C. Gustafson, eds. *Intelligence Elsewhere: Spies and Espionage outside the Anglosphere*. Washington: Georgetown UP, 2013.
(JF 1525 .I6 D39 2013)

Galeotti, Mark. *Russian Security and Paramilitary Forces Since 1991*. Botley, Oxford: Osprey, 2013.
(HV 8227.2 .R8 G35 2013)

Galeotti, Mark, ed. *The Politics of Security in Modern Russia*. Post-Soviet Politics. Burlington: Ashgate, 2010.
(UA 770 .P65 2010)

Greenwald, Glenn. *No Place to Hide: Edward Snowden, the NSA, and the U.S. Surveillance State*. New York: Metropolitan Books/Henry Holt, 2014.
(JF 1525 .W45 G74 2014)

Harding, Luke. *The Snowden Files: The Inside Story of the World's Most Wanted Man*. New York: Vintage, 2014.
(JF 1525 .W45 H37 2014)

Kampfner, John. *Freedom for Sale: Why the World Is Trading Democracy for Security*. New York: Basic, 2010.
(JC 480 .K36 2010)

Keir, Giles and Andrew Monaghan. *Legality in Cyberspace: An Adversary View*. Letort Papers. Carlisle: U.S. Army War College; Strategic Studies Institute, 2014.
(<http://www.strategicstudiesinstitute.army.mil/pubs/display.cfm?pubID=1193>)

_____. *Russian Military Transformation - Goal in Sight?* Letort Papers. Carlisle: U.S. Army War College, Strategic Studies Institute, 2014.
(<http://www.strategicstudiesinstitute.army.mil/pubs/display.cfm?pubID=1196>)

Krickus, Richard J. *Medvedev's Plan: Giving Russia a Voice but Not a Veto in a New European Security System*. Carlisle: U.S. Army War College, Strategic Studies Institute, 2009.
(REPORT LITERATURE   AD-A511 859)
(http://www.strategicstudiesinstitute.army.mil/pdffiles/PUB958.pdf)

Leitenberg, Milton, Raymond A. Zilinskas, and Jens H. Kuhn. *The Soviet Biological Weapons Program: A History*. Cambridge: Harvard UP, 2012.
(UG 447.8 .L45 2012)

McDermott, Roger N., Bertil Nygren, and Carolina Veil Pallin, eds. *The Russian Armed Forces in Transition: Economic, Geopolitical and Institutional Uncertainties*. Routledge Contemporary Russia and Eastern Europe series; 30. London; New York: Routledge, 2012.
(E BOOKS   UA770 .R8184 2012 eb) (EBSCOhost
http://search.ebscohost.com/login.aspx?direct=true&scope=site&db=nlebk&db=nlabk&AN=451258)

Pallin, Carolina Vendil. *Russian Military Reform: A Failed Exercise in Defence Decision Making*. Routledge Contemporary Russia and Eastern Europe Series; 14. London, New York: Routledge, 2009.
(UA 770 .P226 2009)

Thomas, Timothy L. *Recasting the Red Star: Russia Forges Tradition and Technology through Toughness*. Fort Leavenworth: Foreign Military Studies Office, 2011.
(U 163 .T462 2011)

Thornton, Rod. *Military Modernization and the Russian Ground Forces*. Carlisle: U.S Army War College, Strategic Studies Institute, 2011.
(REPORT LITERATURE   AD-A545 442)
(http://www.strategicstudiesinstitute.army.mil/pubs/download.cfm?q=1071)

United States. Congress. House. Committee on Armed Services. Strategic Forces Subcommittee. *Nuclear Weapons Modernization in Russia and China: Understanding Impacts to the United States*. Hearing. 112th Cong., 1st sess. Washington: GPO, 2012.
(Gov Doc Y 4.AR 5/2 A:2011-2012/78)

Ventre, Daniel. *Information Warfare*. London; Hoboken: ISTE; John Wiley, 2009.
(HD 38.7 .V4713 2009)

Woff, Richard. *The Armed Forces of the Former Soviet Union: Evolution, Structure and Personalities*. 2nd ed. London: Brassey's, 1996.
(Reference UA 770 .W49 1996 v.1-3)

JOURNALS

"A Summary of Activities of the US/Soviet-Russian Joint Working Group on Space Biology and Medicine." *Acta Astronautica* 67, no. 7-8(October 2010-November 2010): 649-58.

Baird, Mark A. "Maintaining Space Situational Awareness and Taking It to the Next Level." *Air & Space Power Journal* 27, no. 5(September 2013-October 2013): 50-72.

Faith, G. Ryan. "Future of Space." *World Affairs* 175, no. 3(September 2012-October 2012): 82-7.

Gagnon, Bruce K. "U.S. Space Technology for Controlling China and Russia." *Peace Review* 22, no. 1(January 2010-March 2010): 17-24.

Gottemoeller, R. and BAS. "Rose Gottemoeller: Getting to Yes." *Bulletin of the Atomic Scientists* 67, no. 6(November 2011-December 2011): 1-8.

Graham Jr., Thomas. "The Essentiality of Effective Verification: From Sputnik to the Space Station." *Problems of Post-Communism* 53, no. 2(March 2006-April 2006): 17-29.

Hughes, James H. "Confusion over Space." *The Journal of Social, Political and Economic Studies* 36, no. 1(Spring 2011): 3-54.

Karimova, L, et al. "Power Law Distribution in Statistics of Failures in Operation of Spacecraft Onboard Equipment." *Cosmic Research* 49, no. 5(October 2011): 458-63.

Krasnov, Aleksei. "Risks in International Space Activities." *International Affairs: A Russian Journal of World Politics, Diplomacy & International Relations* 48, no. 4(2002): 68-75.

Logachev, Yu I., L. L. Lazutin, and K. Kudela. "Cosmic Ray Investigation in the Stratosphere and Space: Results from Instruments on Russian Satellites and Balloons." *Advances in Astronomy* 2013(3013): 1-20.

Logsdon, John M. and James R. Millar. "US-Russian Cooperation in Human Spaceflight: Assessing the Impacts." *Space Policy* 17, no. 3(August 2001): 171-78.

Manber, Jeffrey. "Russian--American Space Miscommunication: A Study in Missed Opportunities." *Space Policy* 16, no. 1(February 2000): 3-6.

Moltz, James Clay. "The Past, Present, and Future of Space Security." *Brown Journal of World Affairs* 14, no. 1(Fall 2007-Winter 2007): 187-95.

Pouzanov, S. "Russia-U.S. Space Partnership." *International Affairs: A Russian Journal of World Politics, Diplomacy & International Relations.* 57, no. 1(2011): 238-50.

Yakovenko, A. "The Intergovernmental Agreement on the International Space Station." *Space Policy* 15, no. 2(May 1999): 79-86.

VII. ENVIRONMENT, ENERGY, AND CULTURE
Books, Government Documents, and Report Literature

Baev, Pavel. *Russian Energy Policy and Military Power: Putin's Quest for Greatness.* Contemporary Security Studies. London; New York: Routledge, 2008.
(DK 510.763 .B344 2008)

Balmaceda, Margarita M. *Politics of Energy: Ukraine, Belarus, and Lithuania between Domestic Oligarchs and Russian Pressure.* Toronto: U of Toronto P, 2013.
(HD 9502 .E832 B34 2013)

Balmaceda, Margarita Mercedes. *Politics of Energy Dependency: Ukraine, Belarus, and Lithuania between Domestic Oligarchs and Russian Pressure.* Toronto: U of Toronto P, 2013.
(HD 9502 .E832 B34 2013)

Bartis, James T., et al. *Promoting International Energy Security.* Technical Report; TR-1144. Santa Monica: Rand, 2012.
(REPORT LITERATURE RAND TR-1144/1-AF; RAND TR-1144/2-AF; RAND TR-1144/3-AF)

Bedeski, Robert, and Niklas Swanstrom, eds. *Eurasia's Ascent in Energy and Geopolitics: Rivalry or Partnership for China, Russia and Central Asia?* Routledge Contemporary Asia Series; 38. New York: Routledge, 2012.
(HF 3630.2 .Z7 C628 2012)

Feifer, Gregory. *Russians: The People behind the Power.* New York; Boston: Twelve, 2014.
(DK 510.762 .F45 2014)

Ghaleb, Alexander. *Natural Gas As an Instrument of Russian State Power.* Letort Papers, 51. Carlisle: U.S. Army War College, Strategic Studies Institute, 2011.
(REPORT LITERATURE AD-A551 768)
(http://www.strategicstudiesinstitute.army.mil/pdffiles/PUB1088.pdf)

Gustafson, Thane. *Wheel of Fortune: The Battle for Oil and Power in Russia.* Cambridge: Belknap P of Harvard UP, 2012.
(HD 9575 .R82 G87 2012)

Heinberg, Richard. *Blackout: Coal, Climate and the Last Energy Crisis.* Gabriola Island, BC: New Society, 2009.
(HD 9540.5 .H52 2009b)

Josephson, Paul, et al. *An Environmental History of Russia.* Studies in Environment and History. Cambridge, New York: Cambridge UP, 2013.
(GF 602.7 .J67 2013)

Judah, Ben. *Fragile Empire: How Russia Fell in and Out of Love with Vladimir Putin.*
    New Haven: Yale UP, 2013.
    (DK 510.766 .P87 J83 2013)

Kundu, Nivedita Das, ed. *Russia-India-China: Evolution of Geo-Political Strategic
    Trends.* New Delhi: Academic Foundation in association with Indian Council of
    World Affairs, 2010.
    (DK 510.764 .R8524 2010)

Orbin, Anita. *Power, Energy, and the New Russian Imperialism.* PSI Reports. Westport:
    Praeger Security International, 2008.
    (HD 9502 .R82 O73 2008)

Perovię, Jeronim, Robert W. Orttung, and Andreas Wenger. *Russian Energy Power and
    Foreign Relations: Implications for Conflict and Cooperation.* CSS Studies in
    Security and International Relations. London; New York: Routledge, 2009.
    (HD 9502 .A4 R82 2009)

Slater, Robert. *Seizing Power: The Grab for Global Oil Wealth.* Hoboken: Wiley, 2010.
    (HD 9560.5 .S553 2010)

Wood, John. *Russia, the Asymmetric Threat to the United States: A Potent Mixture of
    Energy and Missiles .* Santa Barbara: Praeger Security, 2009.
    (E 183.8 .R9 W69 2009)

JOURNALS

Blank, Stephen. "Russian Energy and Russian Security." *The Whitehead Journal of
    Diplomacy and International Relations* 12, no. 1(Winter 2011): 173-88.

Brzoska, Michael. "Climate Change and the Military in China, Russia, the United
    Kingdom, and the United States." *Bulletin of the Atomic Scientists* 68, no.
    2(March 2012): 43-52.

Cesnakas, Giedrius. "Energy Security in the Baltic-Black Sea Region: Energy Insecurity
    Sources and Their Impact upon States." *Lithuanian Annual Strategic Review* 10,
    no. 1(2012): 155-97.

Duscha, Vicki, et al. "Costs of Meeting International Climate Targets without Nuclear
    Power." *Climate Policy* 14, no. 3(May 2014): 327-52.

Funke, Odelia. "The Role of Biopolitics in Environmental Security Analysis." *Politics &
    the Life Sciences.* 30, no. 1(Spring 2011): 71-6.

Krass, M. S. "The Electric Power Industry in the Russian Economy." *Problems of
    Economic Transition* 56, no. 4(August 2013): 71-84.

Kubicek, Paul. "Energy Politics and Geopolitical Competition in the Caspian Basin." *Journal of Eurasian Studies* 4, no. 2(July 2013): 171-80.

Kudrin, Alexei. "The Influence of Oil and Gas Exports on Russia's Monetary Policy." *Problems of Economic Transition* 57, no. 1(May 2014): 3-26.

Lachininsky Stanislav Sergeevich. "Russia's Energy Policy in the Baltic Region: A Geoeconomic Approach." *Baltic Region* 16, no. 2(2013): 12-21.

Milina, Velichka. "Energy Security: A Paradigm Shift." *Connections: The Quarterly Journal* 12, no. 4(Fall 2013): 75-97.

Morozov, Yury. "Arctic 2030: What Are the Consequences of Climate Change? The Russian Response." *Bulletin of the Atomic Scientists* 68, no. 4(July 2012-August 2012): 22-7.

Newnham, Randall. "Oil, Carrots, and Sticks: Russia's Energy Resources As a Foreign Policy Tool." *Journal of Eurasian Studies* 2, no. 2(July 2011): 134-43.

Newnham, Randall E. "Pipeline Politics: Russian Energy Sanctions and the 2010 Ukrainian Elections." *Journal of Eurasian Studies* 4, no. 2(July 2013): 115-22.

Shadrina, Elena and Michael Bradshaw. "Russia's Energy Governance Transitions and Implications for Enhanced Cooperation With China, Japan, and South Korea." *Post-Soviet Affairs* 29, no. 6(November 2013): 461-99.

Zeleneva Irina. "Russia's Energy Geostrategy in the Baltic Sea Region." *Baltic Region* 16, no. 2(2013): 4-11 .

Ziegler, Charles E. "Energy Pipeline Networks and Trust: The European Union and Russia in Comparative Perspective." *International Relations* 27, no. 1(March 2013): 3-29.

VIII. ECONOMIC DEVELOPMENT
Books, Government Documents, and Report Literature

Blank, Stephen, ed. *Can Russia Reform? Economic, Political, and Military Perspectives.* Strategic Studies Institute Monograph. Carlisle: U.S. Army War College; Strategic Studies Institute, 2012.
(REPORT LITERATURE   AD-A561 500)
(http://www.strategicstudiesinstitute.army.mil/pubs/display.cfm?pubID=1111)

Hedlund, Stefan. *Invisible Hands, Russian Experience, and Social Science: Approaches to Understanding Systemic Failure.* New York: Cambridge UP, 2011.
(HB 171 .H475 2011)

Oleinik, Anton N. *Market As a Weapon: The Socio-Economic Machinery of Dominance in Russia.* New Brunswick: Transaction, 2011.
(HN 49 .P6 O44 2011)

Robinson, Neil, ed. *The Political Economy of Russia.* Lanham: Rowman & Littlefield, 2013.
(HC 336.27 .P654 2013)

United States. Congress. House. Committee on Foreign Affairs. Subcommittee on Europe and Nonproliferation and Trade. United States. Congress. House. Committee on Foreign Affairs. Subcommittee on Terrorism. *A Relic of the Cold War: Is It Time to Repeal Jackson-Vanik for Russia?* Joint hearing. 111th Cong., 2d sess. Washington: GPO, 2010.
(Gov Doc Y 4.F 76/1:111-112)

JOURNALS

Aganbegian, Abel. "Modernizing Russia's Social System." *Problems of Economic Transition* 54, no. 11(March 2012): 53-72.

Aleksashenko Sergey. "Russia's Economic Agenda to 2020." *International Affairs* 88, no. 1(January 2012): 31-48.

Bandey, Aijaz A. and Farooq Ahmad Rather. "Socio-Economic and Political Motivations of Russian Out-Migration from Central Asia." *Journal of Eurasian Studies* 4, no. 2(July 2013): 146-53.

Baranov, A. O., et al. "The Economic Outlook for Russia in 2012-2014." *Problems of Economic Transition* 56, no. 1(May 2013): 6-21.

Cooper, Julian. "The Russian Economy Twenty Years after the End of the Socialist Economic System." *Journal of Eurasian Studies* 4, no. 1(January 2013): 55-64.

Glaz'ev, S. and G. I. Fetisov. "On a Strategy for Steady Development of the Russian Economy." *Problems of Economic Transition* 56, no. 12(April 2014): 63-76.

Krass, M. S. "The Electric Power Industry in the Russian Economy." *Problems of Economic Transition* 56, no. 4(August 2013): 71-84.

Kudrin, Alexei. "The Influence of Oil and Gas Exports on Russia's Monetary Policy." *Problems of Economic Transition* 57, no. 1(May 2014): 3-26.

Malle, Silvana. "Economic Modernisation and Diversification in Russia:.Constraints and Challenges." *Journal of Eurasian Studies* 4, no. 1(January 2013): 78-99.

Mallea, Silvana. "The Pendulum Moves from Europe to Asia. Modernizing Siberia and the Far East. Economic and Security Issues." *Journal of Eurasian Studies* 5, no. 1(January 2014): 21-38.

McLure, Jason. "Russia in Turmoil." *CQ Researcher* 6, no. 4(February 2012): 81-104. (CQ Researcher Online)

Mel'nikova, L. V. "Growth Prospects for the Russian Economy in Current Long-Term Forecasts." *Problems of Economic Transition* 56, no. 1(May 2013): 41-52.

Oxenstierna, Susanne and Fredrik Westerlund. "Arms Procurement and the Russian Defense Industry: Challenges Up to 2020." *Journal of Slavic Military Studies* 26, no. 1(January 2013-March 2013): 1-24.

Petrakov, N. "On the Question of Modernization of the Economy." *Problems of Economic Transition* 54, no. 7(November 2011): 49-54.

Portanskii, A. "Russia and the World Trade Organization." *Problems of Economic Transition* 55, no. 1(May 2012): 63-77.

Robinson, Neil. "Russia's Response to Crisis: The Paradox of Success." *Europe-Asia Studies* 65, no. 3(May 2013): 450-472.

Shastitko, Audrey. "Antitrust in Russia: To Be or Not to Be?" *Social Sciences* 43, no. 4(2012): 3-17.

Sorokin, Dmitry. "Russia's Development Strategy: Strategy Concept and Economic Reality." *Social Sciences* 42, no. 1(2011): 23-34.

Uziakov, M. N. and R. M. Uziakov. "Key Determinants of a Long-Term Forecast of Russia's Economic Development." *Problems of Economic Transition* 56, no. 10(February 2014): 39-56.

Yakovlev, Andrei. "Russian Modernization: Between the Need for New Players and the Fear of Losing Control of Rent Sources." *Journal of Eurasian Studies* 5, no. 1(January 2014): 10-20.

Zhukovskii, Vladislav. "The Central Bank of the Russian Federation Continues to Block Modernization and Development of the National Economy." *Problems of Economic Transition* 56, no. 9(January 2014): 68-91.

IX. GLOBAL ECONOMIC INFLUENCE
Books, Government Documents, and Report Literature

Aslund, Anders and Gary Clyde Hufbauer. *The United States Should Establish Permanent Normal Trade Relations With Russia*. Policy Analyses in International Economics; 97. Washington: Peterson Institute for International Economics, 2012.
(HF 1456.5 .R8 A75 2012)

Aslund, Anders, S. M. Guriev, and Andrew Kuchins, eds. *Russia after the Global Economic Crisis*. Washington; Moscow: Peterson Institute for International Economics, Center for Strategic and International Studies; New Economic School, 2010.
(HC 340.12 .R8277 2010)

Blum, Douglas W., ed. *Russia and Globalization: Identity, Security, and Society in an Era of Change*. Washington; Baltimore: Woodrow Wilson Center; Johns Hopkins UP, 2008.
(HC 340.12 .R828 2008)

Kundu, Nivedita Das, ed. *Russia-India-China: Evolution of Geo-Political Strategic Trends*. New Delhi: Academic Foundation in association with Indian Council of World Affairs, 2010.
(DK 510.764 .R8524 2010)

Laruelle, Marlène and Sébastien Peyrouse . *Globalizing Central Asia: Geopolitics and the Challenges of Economic Development*. Armonk: M.E. Sharpe, 2013.
(HC 420.3 .L374 2013)

Maswood, Syed Javed. *International Political Economy and Globalization*. 2nd ed. Singapore; River Edge: World Scientific, 2008.
(HF 1359 .M378 2008)

Organisation for Economic Co-operation and Development. *OECD Economic Surveys: The Russian Federation*. Paris: Organisation for Economic Co-operation and Development, 2013.
(http://www.oecd-ilibrary.org/economics/oecd-economic-surveys-russian-federation_19990669)

Popov, Vladimir. *Title: Mixed Fortunes: An Economic History of China, Russia, and the West*. Oxford: Oxford UP, 2014.
(HC 51 .P67 2014)

Robinson, Neil, ed. *The Political Economy of Russia*. Lanham: Rowman & Littlefield, 2013.
(HC 336.27 .P654 2013)

United States. Congress. House. Committee on Foreign Affairs. Subcommittee on Europe, Eurasia and Emerging Threats. *China's Rapid Political and Economic Advances in Central Asia and Russia*. Hearing. 113th Cong., 1st sess. Washington: GPO, 2013.
(Gov Doc Y 4.F 76/1:113-22)

United States. Congress. House. Committee on Ways and Means. *Russia and Moldova Jackson-Vanik Repeal Act of 2012*. Report (to accompany H.R. 6156). 112th Cong., 2d sess. Washington: GPO, 2012.
(Gov Doc Y 1.1/8:112-632)

_____. *Russia's Accession to the World Trade Organization and Granting Russia Permanent Trade Relations*. Hearing. 112th Cong., 2d sess. Washington: GPO, 2012.
(Gov Doc Y 4.W 36:112-25) (http://www.gpo.gov/fdsys/pkg/CHRG-112hhrg80341/pdf/CHRG-112hhrg80341.pdf)

United States. Congress. Senate. Committee on Finance. *Russia and Moldova Jackson-Vanik Repeal and Magnitsky Rule of Law Accountability Act*. Report (to accompany S. 3406). 112th Cong., 2d sess. Washington: GPO, 2012.
(Gov Doc Y 1.1/5:112-226)

JOURNALS

Anand, Aanchal. "Russia in the G20: 'Bearly' Fitting In?" *SAIS Review of International Affairs* 32, no. 2(Summer 2012-Fall 2012): 27-32.

Beary, Brian. "Resurgent Russia." *CQ Researcher* 24, no. 6(February 2014): 121,123-41.

Blunden, Margaret. "Geopolitics and the Northern Sea Route." *International Affairs* 88, no. 1(January 2012): 115-29.

Charap, Samuel and MikhallTroitskiy. "Russia, the West and Integration Dilemma." *Survival* 55, no. 6(December 2013-January 2014): 49-62.

Chornyy, Oleksandr. "Influence of the Bretton Woods Institutions on Economic Growth: Literature Survey for Transitional Economic Systems." *Economics and Sociology* 4, no. 2(2011): 32-41.

Duscha, Vicki, et al. "Costs of Meeting International Climate Targets without Nuclear Power." *Climate Policy* 14, no. 3(May 2014): 327-52.

Ershov, Iu. S. "What Awaits Russia, or Can We Believe Long-Term Economic Forecasts?" *Russian Social Science Review* 54, no. 4(July 2013-August 2013): 76-88.

Jones, Erik and Andrew Whitworth. "The Unintended Consequences of European Sanctions on Russia." *Survival* 56, no. 5(October 2014-November 2014): 21-30.

Kuhrt, Natasha C. "Russia and Asia-Pacific: From 'Competing' to 'Complementary' Regionalisms?" *Politics* 34, no. 2(June 2014): 138-48.

Lieber, Robert J. "The Rise of the BRICS and American Primacy." *International Politics* 51, no. 2(March 2014): 137-54.

Sazonov, A. "Globalization and the Role of the State in Modernizing the Russian Economy." *International Affairs: A Russian Journal of World Politics, Diplomacy & International Relations* 57, no. 3(July 2011): 201-05.

Servettaz, Elena. "A Sanctions Primer." *World Affairs* 177, no. 2(July 2014-August 2014): 82-89.

Szabo, Stephen F. "Germany's Commercial Realism and the Russia Problem." *Survival* 56, no. 5(October 2014-November 2014): 117-28.

Tkalec, Stasa and Marjan Svetlicic. "Can Cooperation with the BRICs and Other Growth Markets Help EU Member States Exit the Crisis?" *Post-Communist Economies* 26, no. 2(June 2014): 176-200.

Zarate, Juan C. "The Coming Financial Wars." *Parameters* 43, no. 4(Winter 2013-2014): 87-97.

Zimin, Dmitry. "How Can Foreign Companies Influence Russia's Economic Course? The Cases of Finnish Firms Fortum and Neste." *Post-Soviet Affairs* 28, no. 2(April 2012-June 2012): 209-31.

X. NUCLEAR AND/OR ATOMIC POLICY
Books, Government Documents, and Report Literature

Alagappa, Muthiah, ed. *The Long Shadow: Nuclear Weapons and Security in 21st Century Asia.* Stanford: Stanford UP, 2008.
(UA 830 .L66 2008)

Arnett, Eric H., ed. *Nuclear Weapons after the Comprehensive Test Ban: Implications for Modernization and Proliferation.* Solna, Sweden; New York: Sipri; Oxford UP, 1996.
(JX 1974.73 .N87 1996)

Blank, Stephen. *Arms Control and Proliferation Challenges to the Reset Policy.* Strategic Studies Institute monograph. Carlisle: U.S. Army War College, Strategic Studies Institute, 2011.
(Gov Doc D 101.146:AR 5)
(http://www.strategicstudiesinstitute.army.mil/pubs/display.cfm?pubID=1085)

Busch, Nathan. *No End in Sight: The Continuing Menace of Nuclear Proliferation.* Lexington: UP of Kentucky, 2004.
(JZ 5675 .B87 2004)

Busch, Nathan E. and Daniel Joyner. *Combating Weapons of Mass Destruction: The Future of International Nonproliferation Policy.* Studies in Security and International Affairs. Athens: U of Georgia P, 2009.
(JZ 5675 .C65 2009)

Cimbala, Stephen J. *Nuclear Weapons and Cooperative Security in the 21st Century: The New Disorder.* Routledge Global Security Studies: 12. London; New York: Routledge, 2010.
(U 264 .C56 2010)

Cimbala, Stephen J., ed. *Deterrence and Nuclear Proliferation in the Twenty-First Century.* Westport: Praeger, 2001.
(U 162.6 .D48 2001)

Delpech, Thérčse and Ros Schwartz. *Iran and the Bomb: The Abdication of International Responsibility.* The CERI Series in Comparative Politics and International Studies. New York: Columbia UP in association with the Centre d'Čtudes et de Recherches Internationales, Paris, 2007.
(JZ 5665 .D4513 2007)

Lodgaard, Sverre. *Nuclear Disarmament and Non-Proliferation: Towards a Nuclear-Weapon-Free World?* Routledge Global Security Studies; 20. London; New York: Routledge, 2012.
(JZ 5675 .L63 2012)

Mathers, Jennifer G. *The Russian Nuclear Shield from Stalin to Yeltsin*. St. Anthony's
    Series. New York: St. Martin's, 2000.
    (UA 770 .M3877 2000)

Ogilvie-White, Tanya, and David Santoro, eds. *Slaying the Nuclear Dragon:
    Disarmament Dynamics in the Twenty-First Century*. Studies in Security and
    International Affairs. Athens: U of Georgia P, 2012.
    (JZ 5675 .S63 2012)

Paul, T. V. *The Tradition of Non-Use of Nuclear Weapons*. Stanford: Stanford Security
    Studies, 2009.
    (U 264 .P38 2009)

Schweitzer, Glenn E. *Containing Russia's Nuclear Firebirds: Harmony and Change at
    the International Science and Technology Center*. Studies in Security and
    International Affairs. Athens: U of Georgia P, 2013.
    (JZ 5675 .S42 2013)

United States. Congress. House. Committee on Armed Services. Strategic Forces
    Subcommittee. *The Current Status and Future Direction for U.S. Nuclear
    Weapons Policy and Posture*. Hearing. 112th Cong., 1st sess. Washington:
    GPO, 2012.
    (Gov Doc Y 4.AR 5/2 A:2011-2012/88)

_____. *Sustaining Nuclear Deterrence after New START*. Hearing. 112th Cong., 1st
    sess. Washington: GPO, 2012.
    (Gov Doc Y 4.AR 5/2 A:2011-2012/58)

United States. Congress. Senate. Committee on Armed Services. *The New START and
    the Implications for National Security*. Hearings. 111th Cong., 2d sess.
    Washington: GPO, 2011.
    (Gov Doc Y 4.AR 5/3:S.HRG.111-897)

United States. Congress. Senate. Committee on Armed Services. Subcommittee on
    Strategic Forces. *Implementation of the New Strategic Arms Reduction Treaty
    (START) and Plans for Future Reductions in Nuclear Warheads and Delivery
    Systems Post-New START Treaty*. Hearing. 112th Cong., 1st sess. Washington:
    GPO, 2012.
    (Gov Doc Y 4.AR 5/3:S.HRG.112-228)

United States. Congress. Senate. Committee on Foreign Relations. *Implementation of
    the New START Treaty, and Related Matters*. Hearing. 112th Cong., 2d sess.
    Washington: GPO, 2012.
    (Gov Doc Y 4.F 76/2:S.HRG.112-652)

JOURNALS

Adamsky, Dmitry Dima. "If War Comes Tomorrow: Russian Thinking about 'Regional Nuclear Deterrence'." *Journal of Slavic Military Studies* 27, no. 1(January 2014-March 2014): 163-88.

Choubey, Deepti. "From Sprint to Marathon: The 2014 Nuclear Security Summit and the Path Ahead." *Arms Control Today* 44, no. 4(May 2014): 16-23.

Cimbala, Stephen J. "Missile Defense Malpractice: U.S.-Russian Relations and Nuclear Fallacy." *Journal of Slavic Military Studies* 25, no. 3(July 2012-September 2012): 269-83.

_____. "Nuclear Arms Reductions after New START: Incremental or Transformative?" *Journal of Slavic Military Studies* 24, no. 1(January 2012-March 2012): 1-25.

_____. "Obama's Second Term: Prospects for Nuclear Arms Reductions." *Journal of Slavic Military Studies* 26, no. 3(July 2013-August 2013): 357-70.

Dabrowski, Richard. "U.S.-Russian Cooperation in Science and Technology: A Case Study of the TOPAZ Space-Based Nuclear Reactor International Program." *Connections: The Quarterly Journal* 13, no. 1(Winter 2013): 71-87.

Diakov, Anatoly and others. "Nuclear Reductions after New START: Obstacles and Opportunities." *Arms Control Today* 41, no. 4(May 2011): 15-22.

Drell, Sidney D. and James E. Goodby. "Nuclear Deterrence in a Changed World." *Arms Control Today* 42, no. 5(June 2012): 8-13.

Goure, Daniel. "Moscow's Visions of Future War: So Many Conflict Scenarios So Little Time, Money and Forces." *Journal of Slavic Military Studies* 27, no. 1(January 2014-March 2014): 63-100.

Harrison, Roger G., Deron R. Jackson, and Collins G. Shackelford. "Space and Defense Deterrence: The Delicate Balance of Risk." *Space and Defense: Scholarly Journal of the United States Air Force Academy Eisenhower Center for Space and Defense Studies* 3, no. 1(Summer 2009): 1-31. http://afac.sdp.sirsi.net/client/search/asset/1027720

Kristensen, Hans M. "Nuclear Weapons Modernization: A Threat to the NPT?" *Arms Control Today* 44, no. 4(May 2014): 8-15.

Kristensen, Hans M. and Robert S. Norris. "Global Nuclear Weapons Inventories, 1945-2013." *Bulletin of the Atomic Scientists* 69, no. 5(September 2013-October 2013): 75-81.

_____. "Nonstrategic Nuclear Weapons, 2012." *Bulletin of the Atomic Scientists* 68, no. 5(September 2012-October 2012): 96-104.

_____. "Russian Nuclear Forces." *Bulletin of the Atomic Scientists* 70, no. 2(March 2014): 75-85.

_____. "Russian Nuclear Forces, 2011." *Bulletin of the Atomic Scientists* 67, no. 3(May 2011): 67-74.

_____. "Russian Nuclear Forces, 2012." *Bulletin of the Atomic Scientists* 68, no. 2(March 2012): 87-97.

_____. "Russian Nuclear Forces, 2013." *Bulletin of the Atomic Scientists* 69, no. 3(May 2013-June 2013): 71-81.

_____. "Russian Nuclear Forces, 2014." *Bulletin of the Atomic Scientists* 70, no. 2(March 2014): 75-85.

Lawlor, Maj Gen Bruce. "The Black Sea: Center of the Nuclear Black Market." *Bulletin of the Atomic Scientists* 67, no. 6(November 2011-December 2011): 73-80.

Mathers, Jennifer G. "Nuclear Weapons in Russian Foreign Policy: Patterns in Presidential Discourse 2000-2010." *Europe-Asia Studies* 64, no. 3(2012): 495-519.

Meier, Oliver and Simon Lunn. "Trapped: NATO, Russia, And the Problem of Tactical Nuclear Weapons." *Arms Control Today* 44, no. 1(January 2014-February 2014): 18-24.

Molis, Arunas and Justina Gliebute. "Prospects for the Development of Nuclear Energy in the Baltic Region." *Lithuanian Annual Strategic Review* 10, no. 1(2012): 121-51.

Ritchie, Nick. "Waiting for Kant: Devaluing and Delegitimizing Nuclear Weapons." *International Affairs* 90, no. 3(May 2014): 601-23.

Savić, Dobrica. "Nuclear Information Democratization." *Online Searcher* 37, no. 6(November 2013-December 2013): 30-51.

Sola, Natividad Fernjndez. "Russia's Non-Proliferation Policy and the Challenges of Rogue Proliferation." *UNISCI Discussion Papers* 30(October 2012): 111-27.

Tannenwald, Nina. "Justice and Fairness in the Nuclear Nonproliferation Regime." *Ethics & International Affairs* 27, no. 3(Fall 2013): 299-317.

Thayer, Bradley A. and Thomas M. Skypek. "Reaffirming the Utility of Nuclear Weapons." *Parameters* 42-43, no. 4-1(Winter 2012-Winter 2013): 41-5.

Wilson, Ward. "Rethinking the Utility of Nuclear Weapons." *Parameters* 42-43, no. 4-1 (Winter 2012-Winter 2013): 35-9.

XI. UKRAINE AND GEORGIA
Books, Government Documents, and Report Literature

Asmus, Ronald D. *A Little War That Shook the World: Georgia, Russia, and the Future of the West*. New York: Palgrave Macmillan, 2010.
(DK 676.9 .R8 A86 2010)

Balmaceda, Margarita Mercedes. *Politics of Energy Dependency: Ukraine, Belarus, and Lithuania between Domestic Oligarchs and Russian Pressure*. Toronto: U of Toronto P, 2013.
(HD 9502 .E832 B34 2013)

Cohen, Ariel and Robert E. Hamilton. *The Russian Military and the Georgia War: Lessons and Implications*. Carlisle: U.S. Army War College, Strategic Studies Institute, 2011.
(REPORT LITERATURE   AD-A545 578)
(http://www.strategicstudiesinstitute.army.mil/pdffiles/PUB1069.pdf)

Kropatcheva, Elena. *Russia's Ukraine Policy against the Background of Russian-Western Competition*. Democracy, Security, Peace; v. 201. Baden-Baden: Nomos, 2010.
(DK 67.5 .U38 K76 2010)

Magocsi, Paul R. *A History of Ukraine: The Land and Its Peoples*. 2nd ed. Toronto; Buffalo: U of Toronto P, 2010.
(DK 508.51 .M34 2010)

Mogocsi, Paul Robert. *This Blessed Land: Crimea and Crimean Tatars*. Toronto: U of Toronto P, 2014.
(DK 508.9 .K78 M34 2014)

Pishchikova, Kateryna. *Promoting Democracy in Postcommunist Ukraine: The Contradictory Outcomes of US Aid to Women's NGOs*. Boulder: FirstForum, 2011.
(JN 6639 .A15 P57 2011)

Rich, Paul B. *Crisis in the Caucasus: Russia, Georgia and the West*. London: Routledge, 2010.
(DK 676.9 .R8 C74 2010)

Thornton, Rod. *Organizational Change in the Russian Airborne Forces: The Lessons of the Georgian Conflict*. Carlisle: U.S. Army War College, Strategic Studies Institute, 2011.
(REPORT LITERATURE   AD-A555 169)
(http://www.strategicstudiesinstitute.army.mil/pubs/display.cfm?pubID=1096)

Trenin, Dmitri. *The Ukraine Crisis and the Resumption of Great-Power Rivalry.* 2014. (http://carnegie.ru/2014/07/09/ukraine-crisis-and-resumption-of-great-power-rivalry/hfgs)

United States. Congress. Senate. Committee on Foreign Relations. Subcommittee on European Affairs. *Georgia: One Year after the August War.* .S. hrg; 111-221. Hearing. 111th Con., 1st sess. Washington: GPO, 2010. (Gov Doc 4.F 76/2:S.HRG.111-221)

JOURNALS

Braun, Aurel. "Tougher Sanctions Now." *World Affairs* 177, no. 2(July 2014-August 2014): 34-42.

Bryce-Rogers, Athena. "Russian Military Reform in the Aftermath of the 2008 Russia-Georgia War." *Demokratizatsiya* 21, no. 3(Summer 2013): 339-68.

Charp, Samuel. "Ukraine: Seeking an Elusive New Normal." *Survival* 56, no. 3(June 2014-July 2014): 85-94.

Charp, Samual and Keith Darden. "Russia and Ukraine." *Survival* 56, no. 2(March 2014): 7-14.

Charp, Samuel. "The Ukraine Impasse." *Survival* 56, no. 5(October 2014-November 2014): 225-32.

Dzebisashvili, Shalva. "Conditionality and Compliance: The Shaky Dimensions of NATO Influence (The Georgian Case)." *Connections: The Quarterly Journal* 13, no. 2(Spring 2014): 1-23.

Fredman, Lawrence. "Ukraine and the Art of Crisis Management." *Survival* 56, no. 3(June 2014-July 2014): 07-42.

Gra, vydas Jasutis. "Forward-Looking Solutions for the Georgian and South Ossetian Conflict: A Path towards Reconciliation." *Baltic Journal of Law and Politics* 6, no. 2(December 2013): 24-49.

Judah, Tim. "The Specter Facing Ukraine." *New York Review of Books* 61, no. 16(October 2014): 78, 80-81.

_____. "Ukraine: The Phony War?" *New York Review of Books* 61, no. 9(May 2014): 41-5.

_____. "Ukraine: What Putin Has Won." *The New York Review of Books* 61, no. 15(October 2014): 56-7.

Kimball, Daryl G. "Arms Checks Unaffected by Ukraine Crisis." *Arms Control Today* 44, no. 3(April 2014): 38-9.

Korostelina, Karina V. "Identity and Power in Ukraine." *Journal of Eurasian Studies* 4, no. 1(January 2013): 34-46.

Kuzio, Taras. "Russianization of Ukrainian National Security Policy under Viktor Yanukovych." *Journal of Slavic Military Studies* 25, no. 4(October 2012-December 2012): 558-81.

Legvold, Robert. "Managing the New Cold War." *Foreign Affairs* 93, no. 4(July 2014-August 2014): 74-84.

Lieven, Anatol. "Ukraine---The Way Out." *New York Review of Books* 61, no. 10(June 2014): 75-6.

MacFarlane, Neil and Anand Menon. "The EU and Ukraine." *Survival* 56, no. 3(June 2014-July 2014): 95-101.

Mankoff, Jeffrey. "Russia's Latest Land Grab." *Foreign Affairs* 93, no. 3(May 2014-June 2014): 60-8.

McFaul, Michael. "Moscow's Choice." *Foreign Affairs* 93, no. 6(November 2014-December 2014): 167-71.

Mearsheimer, John J. "Mearsheimer Replies." *Foreign Affairs* 93, no. 6(November 2014-December 2014): 175-78.

_____. "Why the Ukraine Crisis Is the West's Fault." *Foreign Affairs* 93, no. 5(September 2014-October 2014): 77-89.

Motyl, Alexander J. "Putin's Zugzwang." *World Affairs* 177, no. 2(July 2014-August 2014): 58-65.

Roscoe, Christopher. "Georgia Again in Putin's Shadow." *Connections* 11, no. 2(Spring 2012): 1-4.

Sanders, Deborah. "Ukraine's Maritime Power in the Black Sea—a Terminal Decline?" *Journal of Slavic Military Studies* 25, no. 1(January 2012-March 2012): 17-34.

Sestanovich, Stephen. "How the West Has Won." *Foreign Affairs* 93, no. 6(November 2014-December 2014): 171-75.

Shevtsova, Lilia. "The Russia Factor." *Journal of Democracy* 25, no. 3(July 2014).

Souleimanov, Emil and Maya Ehrmann. "The Armed Incident in Georgia's Lopota Valley and Its Implications for the Security Situation of the South Caucasus." *Connections: The Quarterly Journal* 12, no. 3(Summer 2013): 118-26.

Tonoyan, Artyom. "Rising Armenian-Georgian Tensions and the Possibility of a New Ethnic Conflict in the South Caucasus." *Demokratizatsiya* 18, no. 4(Fall 2010): 287-308.

Umland, Andreas. "Russia's New "Special Path" after the Orange Revolution." *Russian Politics and Law* 50, no. 6(November 2012-December 2012): 19-40.

XII. REFERENCE AND WEBSITES

REFERENCE

Gill, Graeme J., and James Young, eds. *Routledge Handbook of Russian Politics and Society*. Abingdon, Oxen; New York: Routledge, 2012.
(JN 6695 .R693 2012)

Katchanovski, Ivan, et al. *Historical Dictionary of Ukraine*. 2nd ed. Lanham: Scarecrow, 2013.
(DK 508.444 .K64 2013)

Pringle, Robert W. *Historical Dictionary of Russian and Soviet Intelligence*. Historical Dictionaries of Intelligence and Counterintelligence; no. 5. Lanham: Scarecrow, 2006.
(UB 252 .R8 P75 2006)

Weitz, Richard. *Global Security Watch--Russia: A Reference Handbook*. Santa Barbara: Praeger Security International, 2010.
(DK 510.764 .W45 2010)

WEBSITES

Carnegie Moscow Center. carnegie.ru: (copy, paste, click on English).
(carnegie.ru)

REESWEB: World Wide Web Virtual Library for Russian and Eastern European Studies. <http://www.ucis.pitt.edu/reesweb/>.
(http://www.ucis.pitt.edu/reesweb/)

WWW Virtual Library: International Affairs Resources. <http://www2.etown.edu/vl/>.
(http://www2.etown.edu/vl/)

www.ingramcontent.com/pod-product-compliance
Lightning Source LLC
Chambersburg PA
CBHW081537280526
45788CB00010B/3264